Classic Motorbooks

Osceola, Wisconsin 54020, USA

Osprey AutoHistory

FERRARI DINO
206GT, 246GT & GTS

Pininfarina V6 road cars

Osprey AutoHistory

FERRARI DINO 206GT, 246GT & GTS
Pininfarina V6 road cars

IAN WEBB

Published in 1980 by Osprey Publishing Limited,
12–14 Long Acre, London WC2E 9LP

Member company of the George Philip Group
United States distribution by

Publishers & Wholesalers Inc.

Osceola, Wisconsin 54020, USA

British Library Cataloguing in Publication Data
Webb, Ian
Ferrari Dino 206GT, 246GT and GTS. – (Auto
history; 6).
1. Dino automobile
I. Title   II. Series
629.22′22   TL215.D/
ISBN 0-85045-365-8

Editor Tim Parker

Associate Michael Sedgwick

Photography Nicky Wright

Design Giolitto, Wrigley and Couch

Filmset and printed in England
by BAS Printers Limited,
Over Wallop, Hampshire

Contents

Chapter 1
A Company in Transition

For such a small company, Ferrari's products have had a major impact on the world of the motor car. This impact stems directly from motor racing successes, and certainly stimulated courtships by Ford and Fiat in the 1960s. Enzo Ferrari's cars have been at the forefront of grand prix racing for three decades, and while they may not always have been among the winners, they have been favourites whenever enthusiasts have gathered to discuss the subject. Ferrari's have had many glorious years in sports car and grand touring car racing too—always a crucial factor for them in their performance in the road car market, and one which led to their expansion into the 'series' production market.

It is a name instantly recognized by even the most uninterested member of the public. Yet the shrine at Maranello has the capacity, even now, to turn out only about 2000 road cars a year. In 1978 it produced somewhat fewer than the 2000, and to put that into perspective it should be realized that Porsche—their deadly rivals on the other side of the Alps—produced nearly 37,000 new vehicles in the same year, including 5000 of the top line 928 luxury sports cars. This small company was, nevertheless, relatively large in comparison with immediate Italian rivals: between them, Maserati, Lamborghini and De Tomaso made little more than 500 models in the same year.

Left *The most famous racing
car badge in the world but
regretably never placed on a
V6 Dino 206 and 246. It will
only accompany the Dino
script when placed there by a
loving owner*

Above *Ingegnere Enzo
Ferrari, whose son Dino is
commemorated in the cars
that bear his name*

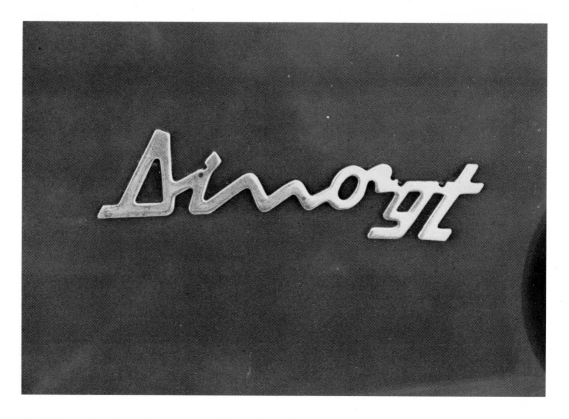

The Dino badge. On early production models Ferrari tried to establish the Dino as a separate marque but soon gave up the unequal struggle and acknowledged the V6 engined cars as the Ferraris they really are

It is hardly surprising, in spite of enormous available wealth. There are almost universal speed limits, all costs have rocketed since the 1973 Arab—Israeli war, and, it must be acknowledged, there has been a backlash against cars that cost as much as most people's houses and are capable of speeds of twice the legal limit. Since the downturn in the economy, the majority of Ferrari's models these days are the smaller V8 cars. There simply is not the demand for the ultra-fast twelve-cylinder cars that created the Ferrari legend.

The twelves will continue to be made, naturally, because there is always a handful of people prepared to pay the asking price for a 180 mph (290 km/h) car with the prancing horse badge on its

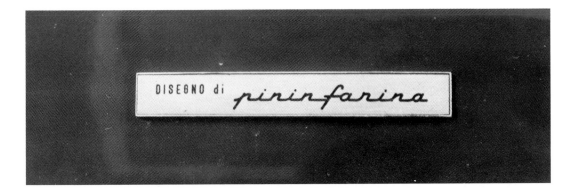

nose. The image was created by them, so the company is safe to withdraw from fielding sports cars in races like the Le Mans 24 Hours. Now, it can concentrate on the all embracing prestige of Formula 1, leaving sports car competition to another province of the Fiat/Lancia empire. Not that many people want to buy Formula 1 cars—though there is a queue, albeit not actually outside the gates of Maranello, for Ferrari's cast-off F1s.

Yet it seems odd to realize that Ferrari's existence as a road car maker rests essentially with a model it launched rather late in life—a model that was created specifically for road use. It came at a low point in the company's history, with the dual purpose of keeping Ferrari in Formula 2 racing, and creaming off some of the burgeoning sales enjoyed by Porsche in the 2-litre category.

The V6 Dino was thus a crucial road car for Ferrari. Had it not been created when it was, the company would have found itself in a near fatal position—much worse than the most uncomfortable period when it actually forged its links with Fiat in 1969. Had it tried to survive alone then, it is unlikely that it could have withstood the rigours and financial demands imposed on all car makers by the energy crisis, not to mention the

Signature of the master; the discreet badge that proclaims Pininfarina-styled bodywork on any Ferrari

9

Not often seen in books about Ferrari, Signor Scaglietti (Senior) is one of the key men in the Dino story. It is in his factory that the bodyshells were built

tightening emission and safety regulations in its one most important export market, North America.

The Dino may have been created for very different reasons, and perhaps no one at the time realized just how vital the model was to prove when the crunch came, in the early 1970s. Then, it was seen as an affordable alternative to the ubiquitous Porsche. It even looked like the little

Dino sports-racing car which had reaped so many rewards on the race tracks of the world, and in the mountain-climb sprints of Europe.

In truth, this was a very different machine under the skin. But it had a lot of racing expertise built in, such as the mid-engine location, the all-independent wishbone suspension, and the low centre of gravity. And though the road car may never have done real battle at the Sarthe circuit,

Dated 1968 this is one of Carrozzeria Pininfarina's Press shots of the 206GT—an all time classic shape

at the Nürburgring, or on the public roads of Sicily, the Dino did have that famous prancing horse on its nose.

Ferrari's approach was the very opposite to that of Porsche. The Ferrari was a road car created with a wealth of racing knowledge built into the design. The Porsche, conversely, was a road car adapted for racing use. It must be acknowledged that Porsche's formula was and is a stupendous success on the race tracks and in the race to the customers. But surely no designer of the time with a blank sheet of paper in front of him would have willingly started from the basis of the Porsche road car, with its torsion bar suspension and an engine hanging out astern.

The philosophies were as far apart as Left and

Galling for the Ferrari Dino owner when he peers beneath the engine cover; most of the Dino castings carry the Fiat name

Right, and like so many extremist views, neither offered a totally satisfactory answer. In the Ferrari's case—the subject of this book—the extravagant, extrovert little Dino was not without its faults. A great many lessons were learned by the company that was accustomed to making few compromises for vehicles to be used on the road. The cars that soon replaced it—the 308GTs with their V8 engine—were altogether different machines.

In the early days the Ferrari was only for the wealthy. It required a king's ransom to buy one, and the kings (and ex-kings) of the world were queueing with the cash. The Dino, on the other hand, was designed to appeal to the younger executive. That meant it had to be cheaper. But its flamboyant styling was perhaps not in keeping with the executive image with which Porsche had so deftly identified.

'It would be hard,' says a fond former owner, 'for anyone to justify ownership of a Dino to an accountant or to an economist. It is unreliable and impractical. A Porsche, on the other hand, is a perfectly acceptable business car. It also has the merit of being able to get an owner to a business appointment on time. The same cannot, unfortunately, always be said of a Dino 246.'

Chapter 2
The Land of Fast Cars

The autostrada from the Brenner Pass on the Austrian-Italian border descends to the Po Valley just by Verona. It then runs for some 100 kilometres (62 miles) due south to Modena, across the flat, fenny, fertile plain that is the larder of Italy. The road is unimaginably dull—a patchwork of highly cultivated fields crisscrossed with grape-hung wires in summer, depressed under a blanket of freezing fog in winter.

Unless you are a fruit-growing member of the National Farmers' Union, excited by the melons and peaches, it is an area to hurry through, on to more interesting places like Florence, Rome and Naples. It is the traditional Italy, though; far from the madding crowds that throng the Adriatic Riviera or the Uffizi Gallery. Apart from the advent of the internal combustion engine, the agricultural methods of the area must be exactly as they were when Rome was ruler of the Mediterranean.

Yet it is also an area noted for its skilled metalworkers—perhaps a tradition that emerged from repairing broken ploughshares and scythes. Today, such people abound as they do in few other areas of the industrialized world, where machine presses and robot welders and automation have closed a chapter of history.

Out of this unexpected background, those attributes have found an outlet in products that

have travelled much further and much more
famously than the Lambrusco wines which the
inhabitants so lovingly create. Today, the crafts-
men are responsible for a handful of cars that
have marked the Italian style—originality, panache, macho, brio—that has been pursued by car
makers the world over.

This is Ferrari country. By the same quirk of
fate, it is also the territory of their adversaries—

*An early precursor—1959
Formula 1 Ferrari Dino
246—with the first script on
the cambox cover*

of Maserati, of Lamborghini, of De Tomaso. These four car factories, and their vital subcontractors, have grown up within a few miles of each other, in a tiny triangle of land that in the field of the automobile is as significant in its way as was the Florentine area a few miles to the south 500 years earlier.

An interchange of personnel between these factories is inevitable. When they go, they carry with them the ideas of their former employers, or ideas of their own which had been badly received. Is it any wonder, then, that the cars they produce should emerge with similar solutions to the same problems?

The list of talented people who have left Ferrari, often after deep-seated rows with the owner, is legion. It embraces Gioacchino Colombo, who went to Maserati; Aurelio Lampredi, who worked later for Fiat and Lancia; and Carlo Chiti, who eventually became head of Autodelta, Alfa Romeo's racing division.

The roads of southern Emilia, Romagna and the foothills of the Apennines have echoed to the screams of V12 engines, the wails of the flat-12s and the thunder of V8s for many years. The toiler in the fields, bent double over the vines, still finds time to admire the test prototypes that disturb an otherwise bucolic way of life. They are proud of a skill that has created such a symphony of moving metal parts.

In fact, the Italians were the first to glorify the car and its speed as far back as 1909—at about the same time as young Enzo Ferrari was being taken to his first motor race by his parents. For the Futurists, the motor car supplanted the Greek gods as symbols of power. F. T. Marinotti, one of its founders, wrote in the manifesto of Futurism, which was published in *Le figaro* that year:

'The world's splendour has been enriched by a

new beauty; the beauty of speed. A racing motor car, its frame adorned by great pipes like snakes with explosive breath ... a roaring motor car which looks as though running on shrapnel is more beautiful than the *Victory of Samothrace*.'

The last reference was to the winged, headless sculpture of the Graeco-Roman period now in the Louvre museum in Paris, a work of art that has inspired a number of other speed-and-beauty emblems.

Serpents and shrapnel may seem a trifle archaic these days, but the manifesto was written before the Great War, when the motor car was in its infancy. Whether the Italian car makers consciously adopted Futurist visions is not clear, but they do seem to have had an amazing influence on the product the customer drives out of the showroom. Just about all Italian cars, even the ones designed for family transport, have a flair for speed and style. The epitome of this must be in the joint creations of Ferrari and Pininfarina, and in the eyes of the true believer none was better than the early Dinos.

This concentration of engineering talent around Modena and Bologna does not exist in many parts of the developed world. The nearest parallel is found in Britain, where automotive efforts have been directed into making racing car chassis, gearboxes, tuned engines and their ancillaries. Like British products, Italian ones make good export business, as wealthy people always seem prepared to part with plenty of money for the best the world has to offer.

Italians' products grew from the same source: the race track. While companies like Daimler-Benz and Alfa Romeo went racing to promote the sales of their passenger cars, Ferrari (and Maserati) went racing because it was in their blood.

More racing heritage but this time a Formula 2 Ferrari at Crystal Palace with Jacky Ickx in the seat. A beautiful racing car

What Ferrari, and the others, found was that there were plenty of aficionados wanting replicas of his racing machines for use on the road as well as on the track. Why not fulfil their wishes, especially if it would subsidize the racing budget?

Those early Italian grand touring models made few concessions to creature comforts. They were noisy, uncomfortable, cramped, under-developed and heavy to steer. They were also fast and thrilling to drive, though, and they were cars that were still capable of winning races against the best opposition in the world. Naturally they would appeal to enthusiasts as road cars.

They also created imitators throughout Europe. High performance grand touring car makers have come and gone, especially in Italy. A few still survive, unsure of the future in these days of the energy crisis and conspicuous consumption that is so widely frowned upon in many countries. In Italy itself, it is even unwise to be seen in a car that suggests the owner is a person of some means.

Makers of high-performance cars faced a bleak outlook in the late 1970s. They had to make concessions to tastes that had been formulated by volume car makers. Who, but a few years ago, could have conceived of a Ferrari with power steering, automatic transmission and air conditioning. Yet it has happened. In the same way that companies like Ferrari influenced the mass producers, so have they made concessions to the niceties introduced by the big battalions.

All of the companies around the Modena–Maranello–Bologna triangle have known their tricky moments, when it was difficult to balance income against increasing outgoings. Ferrari's was in the middle and late 1960s, when their very success on the race tracks attracted the (unwelcome) attentions of the Ford Motor Company of the United States. The takeover very nearly went through.

Maserati, always a smaller concern, faced theirs in the post-1973 energy crisis, eventually to be rescued by one of their rivals, De Tomaso, with a fair amount of state aid. Lamborghini, the newest of the supercar makers, is the odd one out. There are many who believe that its efforts at creating motoring supremes were the match of Ferrari's, which is quite an achievement for a tractor manufacturer with no sporting background. Their flirtation with BMW fizzled out, but the company was rescued in 1979 by a West German consortium.

Ah, but Ferrari—that remains *the* classic car of the postwar years. The comparison with Ettore Bugatti's products between the Wars is inevitable and accurate. It has been suggested by the acceptance of the Ferrari marque into the exclusive Bugatti Owners' Club. Their historical parallels are too plain to ignore. (Today, however, the Ferrari Club flourishes as an independent organization in its own right.)

The Italian-born Bugatti built his cars in small numbers in an area not noted for its industry, at Molsheim in the Alsace region of France. His cars simply looked right, from the outside and under the bonnet. But it was not just a question of style; it was perfection that extended into the very fabric of the car. Bugattis were *the* cars of the 1920s and 1930s; very fashionable, very successful in racing, driven by princes, and admired by paupers.

Ettore Bugatti was a brusque, remote character, loath to change a proven design formula. Furthermore, his son, Jean, who was a leading influence on the design of the later models, was tragically killed in a testing accident in 1939. It was an act which deeply wounded the company's founder. The cars were never the same after the War, and when Ettore died in 1947, the company eventually faded away as a car maker. The name lives on in the many clubs that celebrate the marque, and in the astonishing prices the models command when they (occasionally) change hands.

Is this not a familiar story? Ferraris, built in such tiny numbers to support a motor racing effort, have the postwar panache that Bugatti enjoyed. The image is fostered by the ascetic who heads the company, the withdrawn padrone, who

reportedly has not seen a film or had a holiday for more than forty years. Ferrari, the 'intolerant old martinet', as one observer called him, has kept many a famous customer waiting in the *Cavallino* restaurant for an audience.

This is the Enzo Ferrari who was slow to adapt to new developments like disc brakes, the mid-engine location, petrol injection and light alloy road wheels. It is also the person who so painfully lost his son to the crippling, cruel disease of leukaemia.

The death was such a devastating act of fate that it left the old man deeply aggrieved. So much was expected of Dino, who in his short life had begun to make an impact on the expanding company, especially on the smaller cars. It was in memory of the Ferrari heir that so many of the small cars, and their engines, were given the Dino nameplate.

The shape of the racing Dino, in this case a 206S at the Nürburgring in 1966 driven by Scarfiotti/Bandini, was drawn heavily upon by Pininfarina for what ultimately became the production car

21

Chapter 3
A Father's Tribute to His Son

When Enzo and Laura Ferrari had been expecting their child, Enzo had made the decision to give up his original career as a professional racing driver. He was to be a responsible father to the heir in whom he had so much faith. Enzo Ferrari had lost both of his parents in the War, when he was eighteen, and was determined to give the boy the benefits and guidance he had missed. Alfredo Ferrari—usually known by the affectionate diminutive 'Dino'—was born in January 1932.

Dino proved to be a talented addition to the family. He studied at the local technical institute in Modena, and took an engineering degree in Switzerland, where his thesis explored the design of a $1\frac{1}{2}$-litre engine. Given this background, it was only natural that the should join his father's company. His pet projects were the smaller, six-cylinder machines.

But for all his undoubted skills, Dino was not a fit young man. He spent the last months of his short life in a hospital bed, where he was visited constantly by his father to discuss the progress of the V6 engines that were on the drawing boards at the time. Dino died, in late 1956, never to hear the engines that were to bear his name fired up for the first time. He was twenty-four. Enzo was grief-stricken. Even today, Dino's office is kept as it was when he left for his last appointment. A portrait of

the young man hangs on the wall of the founder's office.

Dino had inherited his father's love of racing—and it is some measure of the old man's love for him that Dino was never allowed to experience first hand what driving on the limit to win is like. But he was positively encouraged to help in the design and development, and was undoubtedly being groomed to fill Ferrari's shoes.

In his memoirs, Enzo Farrari credits his son with much influence on the V6 engines (and a V8) which were to bear his name. But this was more of

This first Pininfarina show Dino, which set the style for the production car, changed little between motor show and manufacture

Rear end treatment, the same 1965 Paris Show car was greeted as a handsome effort

a tribute; he inspired rather than originated the series.

There were three distinct types of V6 Dino, together with a V8; there were as many as twenty-five sub-series; a complicated pattern. First, it should be understood that the naming of these models differed from previous twelve-cylinder practice. In the old system the type number was the capacity of just one cylinder. Thus, a 250 had a 3-litre engine (3000 cc ÷ 12 = 250), a 275 a 3.3-litre, and so on.

In the case of the Dino series, the first two

digits referred to the total engine capacity, and the last to the number of cylinders. The 246 was, therefore, a 2.4-litre six-cylinder engine, and a 308 was a 3-litre eight-cylinder. (Just to complicate matters, while the current 400GT retains the earlier formula, the model commonly known as the Berlinetta Boxer has used both. The 1973 cars were known as 365s, making a capacity of 4.4 litres; when the engine was enlarged to 5 litres in 1976 it became a 512—a 5-litre twelve-cylinder.)

The engine for the road-going Dinos was quite different from earlier racing engines. The first

This early prototype tried putting the engine fore and aft, placing the spare wheel in a position to be alternately baked by the exhaust and grilled by the brakes

type appeared in 1956, and was a 65-degree unit with wet sump lubrication, twin overhead camshafts per bank, and dual ignition. It was intended for Formula 2 racing—which then required a $1\frac{1}{2}$-litre capacity—but in another sub-series was even used in Formula 1. A 120-degree V6 was developed from the same source.

For customers, a single-cam 60 degree V6 with single plug ignition and wet sump lubrication was developed for late 1958. It was, in effect, half of a V12 Testa Rossa engine, and was generally known as the 196.

Nearer still to the production car. Pininfarina's 1966 Turin Show car. The rear glass was a lovely piece of moulding

The third in the series was the one that went into the road cars. It, too, was 65-degree V6, largely the work of engineer Franco Rocchi, who later went on to greater success with the Formula 1 projects. This was an engine intended for Ferrari's idea of volume production, for the regulations of the time called for Formula 2 engines from 1967 to be derived from mass-produced cars.

Enzo Ferrari considered Formula 2 racing vital at the time to foster up-and-coming talent for Grand Prix racing—something he thought was

1967 Frankfurt Show car but really only a styling project with borrowed wings. Fortunately future owners will never know what fiddling with the aerodynamics might have done

sadly lacking in Italy. As far as the racing side is concerned, it was not an outstanding success. The team appeared with a promising array of drivers— Chris Amon, Derek Bell, Ernesto Brambilla, Andrea de Adamich, Jacky Ickx, Brian Redman, Gianclaudio Regazzoni and Mario Casoni—and won precisely nothing in the first year. Neither did they win any Formula 1 races.

In Formula 2 they were outclassed by the four-cylinder Ford-based engines, and it was not until a race at Hockenheim in October 1968 that the Dino won. It was driven by 'Tino' Brambilla— elder brother of Vittorio—who, along with De Adamich, went on to win three of the four races in the South American Temporada series that winter. It was still never a truly auspicious time for Ferrari, however, and when they bowed out of the formula in 1970 and lent a car to Brambilla to run independently, they were never to return to it on a serious, committed basis. These days in racing, Ferrari means primarily Formula 1. But the Dino engine found a new lease of competitive life, in rallying, in another division of the Fiat conglomerate, Lancia. Even getting Ferrari into Formula 2 at that time had been tricky. How could a specialist maker like this produce the 500 units in a year, in addition to its big GT cars, in order to be eligible? For companies like Ford and BMW it was no problem, and indeed they came to dominate the category.

Ferrari's dilemma over the F2 engine came to the notice of Giovanni Agnelli, the head of Fiat, by courtesy of Francesco Bellicardi, the director general of the Weber carburettor firm which was owned by Fiat and a long-time supplier of equipment to Ferrari. At that time there were no formal links between the two companies, for Ferrari was still fiercely independent and Fiat had plenty of problems of its own without wanting to become involved in the cut and thrust of motor racing.

Nevertheless, Fiat agreed to produce Rocchi's engine. It can hardly have been a complete act of altruism on the part of Fiat, but it did allow the two companies to decide whether they liked the look of each other. Despite enormous misgivings on each side—by Ferrari at the prospect of once more having to rely on an outside source for such a vital component, and by Fiat at the thought of having to make an engine for which they had not been responsible and which was probably not even designed for mass-production methods—the V6 was produced in Turin. That it came out of a Fiat factory was plain whenever one of the engines was taken apart; all components were embossed with the Fiat logo, which must have been galling for Ferrari diehards to accept. Fiat soon used a single overhead cam iron-block V6 in their 130 saloon and coupé.

Meanwhile, the now-familiar and distinctive Dino car shape was being evolved on the race tracks too. A 166P sports racing prototype made its debut in the Monza 1000 km in the spring of 1965, driven by Lorenzo Bandini and Giancarlo Baghetti. It lasted only a few laps before the engine blew up with Baghetti at the wheel.

Although this was a pure, lightweight vehicle intended solely for racing, it was a clue to the styling the road-going Dino would adopt. It was a curvy, elegant, mid-engined coupé with a cut-off tail. It even had Dino badges in place of the famous yellow and black Ferrari one. Critics said it was nothing more than a GP car under the GT body.

This racing genre of Dino had a number of successes, and in the following year the 206S appeared. It looked like a miniature version of the now classic 330 P3, which was announced at the same time and rather overshadowed it. It carried a lightweight aluminium alloy body by Piero Drogo of Modena. Like its predecessors, it achieved some notable results, particularly the second place behind the winning Chaparral in the 1966 Nürburgring 1000 kilometres, driven by Bandini and Lodovico Scarfiotti. The car was the talking point of the race—despite it being the American car's first European win, and of the sports car season. It was all good publicity for the road-going model that was being cooked up by Ferrari and Pininfarina.

Already, the public had had a hint of the plans. At the Paris Motor Show of 1965 Pininfarina exhibited a prototype *berlinetta speciale* known as the 206S. This mid-engined car bore more than a passing resemblance to the sports-racing pro-totypes, with its very low roof line—a feature which, it was alleged, restricted occupants to those the size of midgets! Despite the full-width Perspex nose, which covered the driving lights, the shape of the production Dino was being evolved on the race tracks.

By the time of the 1966 Turin Show, Pininfarina's little Ferrari showed a more ob-vious link with the eventual production model. This time it featured the individual recessed headlights in the wings that were to become familiar. It retained the gouged-out air scoops across the flanks that led to the rear brakes, and the exaggerated reverse curve rear screen.

Still experimenting to achieve the optimum shape, at the following year's Frankfurt Motor Show Pininfarina displayed a rather more way-out Dino—strictly speaking, it was still not a Ferrari. It was clearly out of the same stable, but featured the adjustable nose and tail spoilers of the type that were then becoming *de rigueur* in motor racing. Furthermore, it had gull-wing doors and an enormous racing-style double curva-ture windscreen, whose frame was virtually an

upright hoop across the top of the cockpit.

All of these Pininfarina designs bore more than a passing resemblance to the Drogo-bodied racing Dinos of the time and, indeed, with the eventual production Dino. They were all compact, low and curvy two-seaters, some of more pleasing proportions than others. So, when the actual production model made its debut in 1968, ready for sale in Europe, the public had been well primed over what to expect of Ferrari's rival to Porsche—a model itself then four years old.

Not surprisingly, Fiat turned the association to their own advantage too. Those Fiat-made Ferrari engines found their way into a couple of other Dinos—the Fiat variety with conventional front engine and rear-wheel drive.

How to identify a 206GT— triple-eared knock-off hub spinners and the exposed chrome filler cap. Seldom has a road car been so like a racing car

31

A very early brochure dated 7/68 featured the 206 Dino after its V12 brethren. At least the Dino was covered in a Ferrari brochure

DINO 206 GT

ENGINE. Number and arrangement of cylinders: 6 V 65° - Bore and stroke mm 86 × 57 - Piston displacement 1986,61 cc in. - Compression ratio 9 : 1 - Maximum b.h.p. 180 at 8000 r.p.m. - Cylinder block and cranckcase in silumin with forced in liners - Crankshaft on 4 bearings and connecting rods on thin-wall bearings - Inclined overhead valves, operated by 4 camshafts and thimble type tappets - Camshafts driven by 2 silent chains with 2 tensioners - Lubrication by geared pump - Electronic ignition, with switch for normal ignition connection - High tension coil, distributor with automatic advance - Fuel supply by electrical pump and 3 Weber carburettors type 40 DCF - Disc clutch cushion center - Cooling by centrifugal pump, water radiator, expansion tank and automatic electric fan.

CHASSIS. 5-speed rear mounted gearbox operated by a central floor lever - Independent front and rear suspension with transverse wishbones - Worm and peg steering - Left-hand drive - Disc brakes on the four wheels with booster brake, hand-brake on the rear wheels operated by lever - Wheelbase 90 in - Front track 56.1 in. - Rear track 55.1 in. - Empty weight: 1985 lbs - Capacity of the light-alloy fuel tanks: 14.3 Imperial gallons - Fuel consumption 23 miles per Imperial gallon - Cast light-alloy wheels - Tyre size: 185 × 14.

Chapter 4
The Car That Changed a Company

The Italian stylists were part of the motor industry's legend in the 1950s and 1960s. Such names as Michelotti, Vignale, Ghia, Touring, Bertone and Zagoto captured the public imagination with their fresh approach to car shapes. Ideas developed in sharp contrast to the influence being exerted on the other side of the Atlantic. As for the Japanese, they were then still regarded with a certain amount of mirth by the world's car makers. And while the Japanese may not in the end have been able to teach the rest much in the way of car styling, they triumphed in the field of low cost mass production.

But of all the Italian styling houses—so many now gone; Ghia for instance absorbed into the Ford Motor Company fold—none held the centre of the stage quite like Pininfarina. There had always been a close relationship between Sergio and Battista Pininfarina and the man who ran Maranello. Indeed, there were many who were convinced that Pininfarina enjoyed an exclusive contract to create the bodies worn by Ferraris. This was not the case, but it speaks volumes for their working relationship.

The Pininfarina hallmarks of elegance of line, comfort, and good penetration, were certainly exhibited in the Dino prototypes, or styling exercises as they were rather grandly called. The line was flowing and unadorned, apart from obvious necessities like the small, wrap-around rubber-faced bumpers.

'The interrelation between the body of a beautiful woman and that of a Farina-designed car is that both have simplicity and harmony of line, so that when they are old one can still see how beautiful they were when they were young,' said Pininfarina. (As an aside, one wonders whether he considered the young lovelies he created for the BMC Austin, Morris, Riley, Wolseley and MG saloons of the late 1950s to have stood the test of time like some of the more exotic exercises for companies like Ferrari!)

The real question is whether the widespread enthusiasm for the look of the Dino evolved from what it was, or from what it represented in ambition, fantasy or envy in the mind of the viewer. The person who loves speed and sport cannot dissociate in his mind the image of what he sees, with that of a car from a company that has won so many motor races. Is it simply a beautiful shape, or does the attraction lie in what the shape represents? A non-car enthusiast with an eye for beauty has difficulty distinguishing the Dino from any one of a clutch of similarly low-slung, fast cars.

However, when the Dino 206GT made its debut in the late autumn of 1967 it was greeted with a mixture of admiration and scepticism. It was widely held to be a very fine looking machine, the first of the company's road cars to feature a power unit amidships like the new generation of racers. But it was a 2-litre from a company that had been producing powerful 3-litre models. Would the public take to it?

Perhaps Ferrari was aware of the possible problem too, for nowhere on the newcomer was the company's badge displayed. Instead, it was known simply as a Dino, with script to that effect on the nose and on the camshaft covers. No one

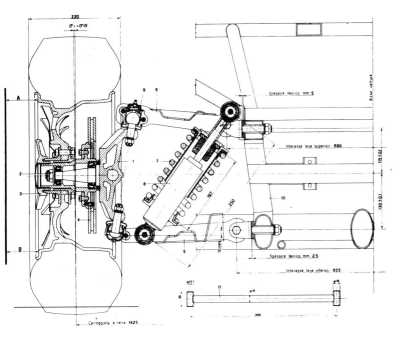

A conservative company despite its image, Ferrari were happy to give the Dino conventional pressed steel wishbones and slender brake discs at the front. The drawing seeks to inform an owner, being taken from the driver's handbook

was fooled, of course—it was just a small Ferrari.

However beloved the memory of Dino, his name could not compete with the family's. Besides, anyone wanting to buy a model made in the Ferrari works, and prepared to part with a lot of money for it, expected that prancing horse badge to be there. There was some woolly-headed theory that the little V6 would in some way detract from the twelves that the company was making, but anyone who drove those early models knew the mystique was secure.

Ferrari's answer to the Porsche was a complete contrast to it. It carried those curves that had been evolved from the racing days and brought immediate oohs and aahs from the *cognoscenti*. Yet it appeared at a time when most Italian stylists were moving towards the straight lines and wedge shapes that Giugiaro would exploit so tellingly. To that extent, the Dino became dated in style quite quickly, with the result that today it looks like the 1960s car it basically is, rather than a product of the 1970s.

The slippery, low-drag shape featured a small, oval air intake at the front, flanked by recessed headlights in the large front wings. The windscreen was steeply raked, the roof line low and the rear pillar fillets swept down towards the cut-off Kamm-style tail. The rear screen featured the vertical reverse curve seen on the show cars—and it was an altogether much tidier treatment than Jaguar's own solution to the problem when designing the XJ-S several years later. The large wheel arches gave the car a distinctly waisted look, and it retained the air intake recesses in the tops of the doors. The doors were very large and opened conventionally. Production of the body was the work of Scaglietti, using aluminium alloy.

The Dino stood on light alloy Cromodora

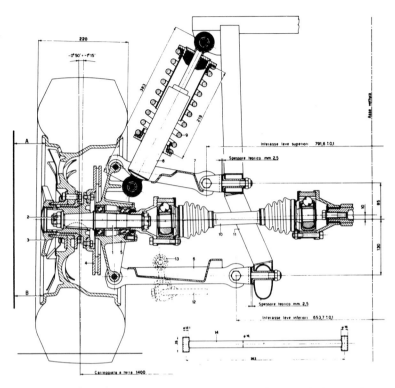

Pure racing heritage is emphasised in the double wishbone and coil spring rear suspension. The photograph is of a 246, the drawing of a 206 as is the case with the previous pair of illustrations

37

One of the several snags with a mid-engined car; the engine is extremely inaccessible

wheels—a Fiat economy influence since the more expensive Ferraris used Campagnolo's costly units. They were 14 inches in diameter and carried 185 × 14 tyres.

Suspension was by unequal length wishbones and coil springs front and rear, both ends equipped with anti-roll bars. Brakes featured vacuum servo assistance and twin circuits for safety. Naturally, there were ventilated discs all round, 11 inches diameter at the front and 10.5 inches diameter at the rear.

The steering was by rack and pinion, with a nice three and a quarter turns lock to lock. This in itself was a departure for Ferrari, all of whose previous road cars had used the worm and peg steering mechanism. The radiator was located up front as well, aided by an electric fan. The space under the bonnet was largely occupied by the spare wheel, leaving the boot luggage area free from obstruction.

The chassis for the vehicle was a substantial ladder frame made from oval- and rectangular-section tubes. It carried further tubular steel superstructures fore and aft. In all, it was not a terribly sophisticated looking piece of work, but it did seem to work extremely well.

Rocchi's V6 engine was turned sideways in the chassis to save space. This left a reasonable amount of room behind the engine and above the rear suspension for a completely carpeted luggage space. Both were reached via a couple of lids with releases set in the offside door frame.

The all light alloy engine—made by Fiat in Turin and installed at the Maranello works—featured twin overhead camshafts per bank, driven by primary reduction gears and chains. The valves were actuated directly via bucket tappets. The engine had a bore and stroke of 86×57 mm for a capacity of 1987 cc.

Equipped with three downdraught Weber 40DCF carburettors, and running on a compression ratio of 9.3:1, it produced 180 bhp at 8000 rpm. Power was taken via a diaphragm spring clutch through a series of three pinions to the primary shaft of the five-speed, all-synchromesh gearbox. This was alongside the crankcase and fed the limited slip differential through a pair of spur gears. In this manner the driveshafts ran in parallel with the crankcase.

Inside, occupants sat in semi-reclining positions, exposed to the stares of passers-by because of the large amount of glass and the low build of

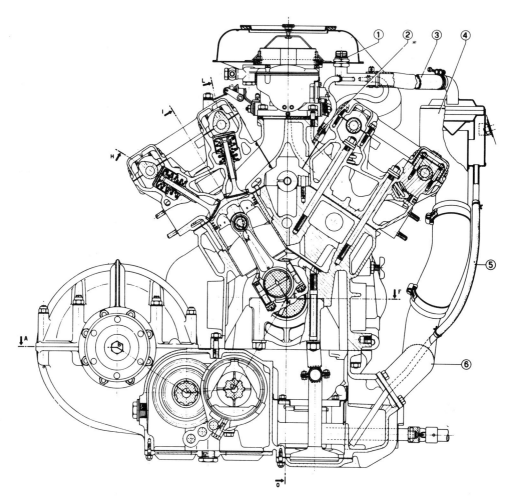

*Another superb drawing
from a driver's handbook
captioned in three languages.
Designed to show crankcase
ventilation it shows nicely
the crankcase/transmission
relationship*

the body. There was full instrumentation in front of the driver, and just about enough space behind the seats for a briefcase. The facia was trimmed in a fake suede-like material which was non-reflective and looked very smart. It featured electrically operated window lifts (standard when the car was imported to the UK), full carpeting and a usable luggage compartment. It was all a far cry from the so-called road cars that up until then had been made by the company.

About as hand-made as a car can be, the Dino has a crankshaft which gets the same loving, tender care from the machinists as any V12 crankshaft

The techniques of volume car production have always been happily ignored at Ferrari, with engine assembly as with every other aspect of car construction carried out almost entirely by hand

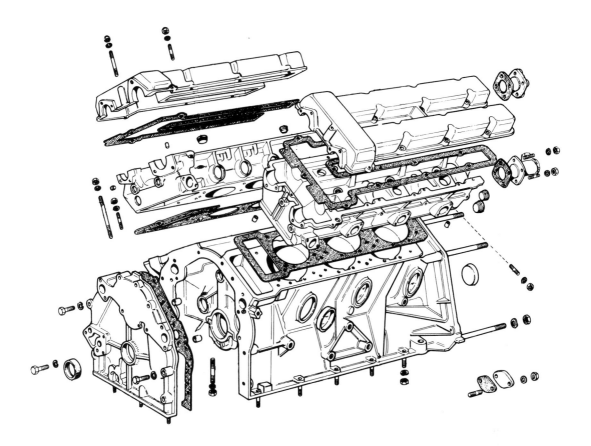

It was also something of a 'bitsa': a Ferrari-designed engine made by Fiat, a body styled by Pininfarina of Turin and turned into metal by Scaglietti of Modena, with the final assembly at the Ferrari works of Maranello. By Ferrari standards, this was a production car, and one that even necessitated construction of an extra wing at the factory just to make the Dino. It still featured relatively few bought-in components, apart from obvious items like the Webers and Cromodoras, in which the company had complete faith.

One problem was immediately obvious. The

Nothing if not complex, the 2·4-litre twin cam V6 probably set new records in complication for an engine of this size. High power and relatively good engine life have to be paid for

206 was not quite fast enough to match the latest Porsches. So after only 150 had been built, it was replaced by a 2418 cc version, achieved by increasing the bore and stroke to 92.5 × 60 mm. This took the power to 195 bhp at 7600 rpm, but more importantly it improved torque considerably. Ferrari has sometimes been a little coy about revealing torque figures but the 246, as it was called, had 165.5 ft lb at the very high crankshaft speed of 5500 rpm.

The 246 appeared in the spring of 1969. This was the version which found its way to the United States in 1970, but by then the emission requirements had reduced the US model's power output to a mere 175 bhp.

The larger 246 differed from its predecessor in a number of significant ways. While the 2-litre engine blocks were made of light alloy, the 'production' ones were made of cast iron. Similarly, the light alloy bodywork of the 206 gave way to a thin steel one in the 246. It, too, was hand-beaten at the Scaglietti works. Owners claim it is quite easy to tell they were hand-made—no two ostensibly identical panels were quite the same!

The early 206 models—the few that were actually imported into the UK—were in left hand drive form only. With the introduction of the 246, right-hand drive became available. Those models destined for the UK had electrically operated window lifts as standard, whereas in many markets they were an extra. The plastic light covers seem to have been another British peculiarity too.

While they may have added another 1 mph to to the top speed and, more subjectively, improved the racy lines, they were unpleasant to use on a wet night. The Dino's lights were never notably good, and the diffusion caused by the clear plastic and the rain drops on them did nothing to improve

At a relatively late stage in production, engine and gearbox/final drive were mated to form a single unit

the driver's vision as he thundered into the British countryside at night.

The 246's height was increased by three inches over the 206, and there were small changes to the car's other dimensions. Larger section tyres were used on the later models—205 × 14 in place of the 185 × 14. The fuel tank (101 octane was the recommended grade) gained another gallon in capacity to reach 14½ Imperial gallons (66 litres).

This gave the 246 an absolute range of around

290 miles (470 km) on a tank of petrol, depending on the type of driving indulged in. The maximum owners seemed to coax out of the 246 was around 20 mpg, but if a driver wanted to enjoy a bit of that Ferrari magic it could soon drop to 16 mpg, or a range of little more than 230 miles.

Eventually, the 246GT weighed in at 2380 pounds (1079.5 kg), all of which gave a speed in excess of 145 mph (233 km/h) compared with around 140 mph for the small one. Some road tests of the time spoke of 150 mph-plus top speeds being achieved by the 2.4, but clearly, accurate checking of such velocities was a bit tricky—and academic anyway. Needless to say, it was mightily quick by most people's standards, and plenty quick enough even for enthusiasts as speed limits began to close in around the world.

The model continued in this basic form until its replacement by the 308GT4 in 1973. The only addition to the 246 story came at the Geneva Motor Show in the spring of 1972, when an open Targa-type known as the GTS was introduced. This boasted a removable roof panel which could be stowed behind the seats to provide open-air motoring. The rear three-quarter window disappeared, to be replaced by a more substantial, solid roll-over type of hoop which replaced some (but not all) of the torsional stiffness lost by the removal of the roof panel. Otherwise, the two models remained exactly the same until their demise.

The Dino represented a marked expansion in Ferrari road vehicle output. The company's first model was sold to a customer in 1947. Even by the 1950s, annual production never reached more than eighty. By 1960 it was up to 300, and by 1965 some 750 units a year were sold. Clearly there was little slack to make sudden production increases just to meet the demands of the 1.6-litre Formula 2

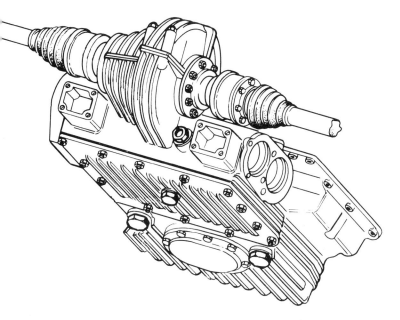

Other manufacturers might have used a pressed steel sump instead of a casting to complete this otherwise complex final drive casting

Until fuel injection was introduced most Ferrari engines from the early 1960s used one choke per cylinder with Weber carburettors

regulations which called for a minimum of 500 units to be produced annually. . . .

But the addition of the Dino, courtesy of Fiat, added a new dimension to Ferrari's record as a road car maker. In 1970, early in the Dino's production run, the factory gained another 100,000 square feet of space to add to the existing 170,000 square feet. It was all turned over to the production of the Dino.

At its peak, Dino production reached 1000 units annually—yet this was still not enough to satisfy demand. When production eventually ceased, 2732 versions of the 246GT had been

produced in the six years previous to the end of 1974. The total for the open GTS version stood at 1180, which was achieved in just three years.

Clearly, keeping that engine production line open for such a small demand did not make good financial sense to Fiat. Not surprisingly, they turned the association to their advantage by producing their own Dinos. Like its more exotic cousin, the early ones had the 2-litre all-alloy engine, tuned to produce 165 bhp. Then, in 1969, with the Ferrari model already established, the Fiat was given the 2.4-litre engine with cast iron block. In Fiat's case, it was tuned to

Complex-looking but actually quite simple jigs were used by Scaglietti to produce a correctly aligned chassis/ body

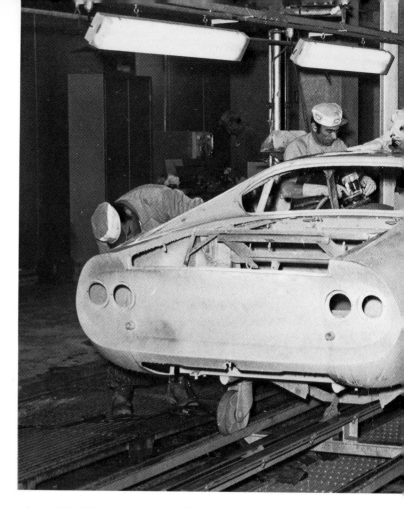

give 180 bhp—some eight per cent less than the Ferrari—though the only differences were said to be carburettor settings.

More importantly, the Fiat Dino with the larger engine received an independent rear suspension system in place of the (admittedly sophisticated) live rear axle of the 2-litre. It was a coil sprung unit with semi-trailing arms. It also gained a limited slip differential. The Fiat was capable of speeds in the region of 130 mph or more, and took very little time to get there. On a cross-country A–B journey, the Fiat Dino, particularly the 2-seater, would be very nearly a match for the Ferrari.

Two versions were made; a four-seater coupé styled by Bertone, and an open two-seater with bodywork by Pininfarina. Again, the swooping wheel arches and waisted look in this otherwise conventional car bore more than a passing resemblance to the Ferrari Dino and other Pininfarina works. None were ever 'officially' imported to the UK, and those that are here will certainly have left-hand drive.

All of this activity occurred at a time when Fiat was busy buying into Ferrari. When the links were being forged—in the late 1960s—there were at first no normal ties. Ferrari was going through

About as close to a production line as the Dino got during its assembly, which started at the Scaglietti works in Modena for chassis/body construction, moved to Maranello for mechanical installations and then back to Scaglietti for finishing

a lean spell on the race tracks, even if sales of the road cars had never been better. But profits on those were nowhere near enough to sponsor the company in so many types of racing, and there were expensive plans to be laid if the company was to get back in to the forefront of motor racing.

Few people know how much money was sunk into Ferrari following the stark press announcement on 21 June, 1969. It came, ironically, in the middle of a disastrous year for the competition division, with precious few wins in any of its many categories. Fortunes have certainly changed since then, both on the road car and racing front.

The current 308 Dinos, and other Ferraris, are considerably more developed and reliable than their predecessors, thanks largely to Fiat control. The racing team, with the old man still at its head, concentrated on Formula 1 with such success that it won the World Championship series in four years out of five, up to 1979.

Not all of this came about as a result of the Dino story; it would possibly have happened in any case. It is certain, though, that the Dino experience acted as a catalyst in bringing together two fine companies which, up to that point, had probably not realized they needed each other.

Chapter 5
Driving the Legend

All at Ferrari are racing enthusiasts. They expect their customers to be so too. There have been compromises over the years, but driving a Ferrari is unlike driving so many other sporting machines of a similar price, and that includes cars built by Porsche, BMW, Jaguar and Daimler-Benz. In such cars the driver and occupants are, to a greater or lesser degree, cocooned from the world about them. Years of engineering know-how have eliminated the irritants which might have jarred on the owner's nerves. This is not the way Ferrari builds cars.

Tremendous thought went into the Dino too, but the emphasis was put, instead, on making it go quickly—round a bend and in a straight line—and on enabling the driver to feel safe and positive when doing so. The creators wanted it to stop well, and to carry two people and a small amount of luggage. Everything else was secondary.

It may have been an improvement on the boneshakers of yesteryear, but judged against the vehicles of its age it was one of the least compromising cars around. The late Michael Parkes, the Englishman who raced for Ferrari and eventually became an engineer there, made tremendous strides in getting the company to make cars that were less demanding to drive, more comfortable to ride in and generally more civilized for road use. The Dino stood at a point of transition,

Right
The first Dino 246GT brochure dated 9/69. Featuring a 206GT in all the illustrations tells its own story as does 'Tiny, brilliant, safe . . . almost a Ferrari'

54

Minuscola, scattante, sicura… quasi una Ferrari
Minuscule, verveuse, súre… presque une Ferrari
Tiny, brilliant, safe… almost a Ferrari

Cockpit, flight deck or just simple dashboard—whatever the term, you are told several times that you are in control of a Dino

for it was still underdeveloped and underproduced by the standards of the day.

Sliding into the hammock-like seat—trimmed in none too luxurious black plastic—is like living out a racing fantasy. This, to most people, is Walter Mitty land, emphasized by the small, leather-rimmed Momo steering wheel, the full set of Veglia instruments complete with an optimistic 170 mph speedometer, and the gear lever for the five-speed box with its racing-type open gate. The pedals, slightly offset because of the wheel arches, are perfectly placed, and there is that essential footrest by the side of the clutch for use when cornering or braking hard.

A twist of the ignition key and those six beautifully forged alloy pistons come dancing to

Finally the 246GT with petrol filler flap over the screw cap and five-stud bolt on wheels. A Pininfarina Press photograph

life. The rev counter points out the tale like a studio sound meter recording the audience's applause. The burble turns into a tenor whine as the Webers suck more air and petrol into the machine.

The straight-arm driving position gives a good view of the road ahead, flanked by the enormous curves of the front wheel arches. The driver can see nothing of the nose, which makes him a bit circumspect as he filters into the traffic for the first time. It takes many hundred miles to learn how to drive a fast car like a Dino properly. And until those miles have been swallowed by the low-slung machine, the driver gingerly changes gear, pussyfoots around bends and accelerates only when there is a clear, open road ahead.

57

But once the practice period is over, the Dino driver is king of the road. He begins to learn the limits of its adhesion—almost always beyond his own skill in handling it—and to make better use of nearly 200 bhp in a slippery car weighing in little over a ton.

Put a few thousand revs on the tachometer, easing the clutch out, and the car squats for a fraction of a second before blasting up the road.

The rev counter needle is up to the red line in a few seconds, and then it's the tricky change to second: forward and to the right alongside reverse. Giving the accelerator its rightful position on the floor once more, the car bounds up to a blurred 60 mph. Just over seven seconds have passed since the clutch began to bite.

There is a steady, hefty shove in the small of the back and the rise and fall of the engine with

A classic among postwar cars and quite one of the finest of line from Ferrari. Here is one of the UK importer's Press cars photographed by Neill Bruce for Maranello Concessionaires at Wentworth

The Spider version of the Dino caught on immediately and has subsequently become even more of a collector's item than the coupé

Ferrari
SOCIETÀ RER AZIONI ESERCIZIO FABBRICHE AUTOMOBILI E CORSE
CAPITALE SOCIALE UN MILIARDO

Rimesso № 437 **V**

Spedizione fatta da Maranello Modena il 9/12/70

in porto ....

merce affidata a Mr. MASON STYRRON

nostro riferimento ....

Ordine ....

del 17/6/70

Spett.le
MARANELLO CONCESSIONAIRES LTD
Tower Service Station
EGHAM BY PASS - SURREY

DESCRIZIONE DELLA VETTURA

N. 1	VETTURA FERRARI MATRICOLA FERRARI CAR. SERIAL NUMBER.	MOTORE 01252 ENGINE TELAIO 01252 CHASSIS	TIPO TYPE	DINO 246/GT

CARROZZATA BODY COUPE

COLORE ESTERNO OUTSIDE COLOR ROSSO CHIARO FERRARI 20 - R - 190 SALCHI

FINITURA INTERNA INSIDE UPHOLSTERY PELLE NERA N/P E PELLE ROSSA 101

TACHIMETRO Km. □ MIGLIA
SPEEDOMETER in Km. □ MILES X

CORREDATA DI OUTFIT

N. 5 RUOTE WHEELS IN LEGA 14/6½

GOMMATE TYRE MICHELIN 205/70 VR 14

N. 1	BORSETTA ATTREZZI NORMALI TOOL KIT	N. 2	CINGHIE PER PILOTA e passeggeri DRIVER BELT	
N. 2	SERIE CHIAVI per CRUSCOTTO E PORTIERA SET OF KEYS FOR DASHBOARD	N.	CINGHIE FISSAGGIO VALIGIE LUGGAGE BELT	
N.	POGGIATESTA HEAD REST	N. 1	BARATTOLO DI VERNICE TIN OF PAINT	
N.	RADIO	N.	SPEED PILOT	
N. 1	CINGHIA per VENTILATORE FAN BELT	N. 2	PORTATARGHE NUMBER PLATE HOLDER	

VETRI ELETTRICI - Kg. 3 DI VERNICE - BUSTA PELLE PORTADOCUMENTI - TESSERA DI GARANZIA
N° 531/D - BOLLA DOGANALE A55 N° 1857 DEL 4/12/70

NATURA DELL'IMBALLO	DA FATTURARE :	A RENDERE :	A PERDERE :
CREDIT 1.882.697/D	2431/70		
COMPILATO DA : RV	CONTROLLATO DA :	CONTABILITA :	USCITA :

AM - cat. 80 - n. 1000 - 2/70

The paperwork required when a customer went to Modena to pick up his new Dino in 1970. 01252 must have been a very early 246GT with right-hand drive

With the GTS, Ferrari achieved open car motoring without sacrificing too much body stiffness once having cut a hole in the roof. These cars worked very well when the weather was good

the gear changes. With an open road before it, the Dino pulls quickly up the speed range. A glimpse of the road disappearing under the facia between those two rounded wheel arches, and the driver could be flying at full speed along the Le Mans Mulsanne straight. It is all happening so quickly.

A fast bend—it could be the Parabolica at Monza—requires a flick of the wrist on the little wheel. The Dino just goes round, sucked on to the tarmac, with no roll whatsoever and sure-footed to the nth degree. It is like mind over matter: the driver simply looking down his arm and into the

Rock steady at an indicated 130 mph. These are Autosport *road tester John Bolster's hands on the wheel*

corner and willing the car to go round at speeds unimaginable in ninety-nine per cent of other road cars.

John Bolster, writing of his experiences with a Dino 246GT in *Autosport* in 1971, says: 'On the open road the Dino is an absolute delight. The performance depends largely on intelligent use of the gearbox, which is as it should be for this type of car. One has to control wheelspin on first gear, of course, but the traction is exceptional and the

inside tyre never spins on corners. The engine is completely smooth and utterly effortless through its range, being at least the equal, in this respect, of the 12-cylinder Ferraris, incredible though this may seem.'

The country road unwinds, deserted of traffic, dry and with perfect vision. The driver gets into his stride, with firm braking and strong acceleration, reading the road ahead and snicking into gears. The gearbox, guided by its open frame

Not the same speed but the same car and driver. John Bolster reported in favour of this Ferrari

63

A rare shot of a Dino racing (or spinning). This time it's Brands Hatch in 1979

gate, is uncannily good. It feels a little stiff at first, but once warmed up it is positive and precise. It is spring-loaded in the fourth-fifth plane, so that even a staggered change like that from third to fourth is as precise as turning on a light switch. It is either on or off, in third gear or fourth.

The Dino responds instantly to the driver's hands, and with a quick left and right the driver could be in Collesano High Street, leading the Targa Florio. That Cortina ahead suddenly becomes Stommelen's Porsche, and there are only a few kilometres to go on the final lap.

With ease, the Dino hauls in the leader, braking harder and later, then getting back on to

Above *How the road car shape was made. Timeless beauty from this 1966 ex-works 206SP Dino*

Left *The Dino badge is right, the Prancing Horse is an owner's respectful addition*

Above *206GT — readily distinguishable with its knock-on hubs and 'crude' filler cap*

Right *The same 206, one of only a handful in Britain*

Far right *Not a colour normally associated with Ferrari, Dino 246GTs often came in their Italian silver*

Left *'Dino' on the steering
wheel boss and instrument
faces — 246GT in England*

Above *Note the change in
wheel hubs and the way the
filler cap is covered — 246GT*

Right *Not often raced because the Porsche 911 was more adaptable, but still competitive in the right place. This Turin registered 246GT ran the Targa Florio*

Below *246GTS, thought by many to be the best of all the Dinos. Some have said that the car suffers when the roof is cut off!*

Above *Yet another Dino
colour which pleases because
the line of the car is so
delightful. 246GTS at
Goodwood during an Owners'
Club outing*

Left *Scaglietti's paint shop in
1973. A yellow Daytona
follows the red Dino*

the loud pedal in the twinkling of a Fred Astaire footstep. Down a dip, pull out to look, and blast by, sending shock waves to the Cortina driver, who is sawing at the steering wheel in disbelief. The Dino was not there when he looked in his mirror less than a minute ago—and it is not there now, five seconds later.

The driver can hold a perfect line through any smooth bend—and amazingly well when the road is a bit bumpy—and at the very limit all four wheels edge gingerly, imperceptibly to the outer edge of the radius. The limit is reached, and those Michelins are sliding ever so gently in unison across the tarmac.

Up and over a crest, the car momentarily takes off—like Brunnchen at the 'Ring in the good old

246GTS at speed on the Goodwood racing circuit during one of the English Ferrari Owners' Club outings

Far left The V6 Dino engine has lived on in the Lancia Stratos although sadly it is no longer made. A rare shot of a racing Stratos on the 1973 Targa Florio with Sandro Munari and Jean-Claude Andruet

73

days—and into a slow, tricky hairpin. It is like Spa's La Source, and the driver could swear that he caught a glimpse of the spectators in the terrace café as he powers the car down the hill.

Towards where? Not to the pits, but to reality. The Dino may not have been a racing car, but it has so much racing ethos built into it that it is all too easy for the driver to dream. The Dino is not an effete machine that simply looks good. It is an aristocrat in an age of increasing meritocracy, but like the thoroughbred it is, it comes out on top of that scale too. It is, as the late Ken Purdy wrote, 'An example of the purest expression man has been able to give to the age-old wish to move privately, speedily and elegantly over the face of the earth' (*Ken Purdy's Book of Automobiles*, Cassell).

Paul Frère, the noted Belgian writer and former Ferrari team driver, told *Motor* readers in 1969 of his first experience with a Dino, then the 206: 'The noise is mainly mechanical, and no amount of soundproofing material will ever be able to conceal the fact that a twin-cam engine revving at 8000 rpm driving a five-speed gearbox through a set of three transfer gears is only a matter of inches away from one's ears. Whether this noise ... is really objectionable or not must be up to the user.'

The speed and manner of its going are most impressive for a 2.4-litre car, and the 2-litre before it. It feels rock-steady at very high speed, and exhibits a splendid absence of noise from the tyres and from the passage of air over the aerodynamic body

Frère noted that the factory had no press fleet test models available, even for those who had once been entrusted with racing cars. The car that Frère drove was on loan from Sergio Pininfarina, who, it seemed, has also been called upon to loan it to Umberto Agnelli, Gianni's brother and then a Fiat

An American specification Dino 'supremo' with recessed indicator lamps and side marker lamps

vice-president, and to the Fiat Experimental department. It is one of the reasons why published road tests of Ferraris are rather rare. The tester had then to beg one from a dealer or friend, or even, in certain extreme cases, buy one! Again, it is all part of an official factory attitude that has fuelled the Ferrari myth.

Driving a Dino is not something that everyone would appreciate. It could only appeal to someone who has a sympathy and love for the metal parts that form the modern-day classic. Its road holding and handling characteristics would be lost on so many motorists, who could only draw their breath through their teeth in total disbelief at the costs involved in buying and owning one.

It amounts to the sort of perfection that commands such high prices whenever great conductors take up the baton, whenever a painting of a master comes under the hammer. Driving the Dino, one begins to appreciate the accuracy of those Futurists seventy years ago. Vehicles like the little Ferrari must surely go down as a 20th century art form.

Chapter 6
Living With the Legend

That is the good part. Anyone who has owned a Dino, or even driven one for a modest distance, will soon confirm that there are plenty of drawbacks.

It becomes apparent very rapidly that providing fresh air ventilation for the passengers was not one of Ferrari's priorities. It is stiflingly hot inside even with the controls adjusted to maximum cool, and in anything but mid-winter most owners will insist on travelling with the windows

It has proven impossible to be accurate as to the time, place and actual Formula 1 Ferrari in this photograph but it does illustrate that the Dino is every inch a racing car for the road even when compared with a Grand Prix winner. Function has its own beauty

77

open. Thoughtfully, and in typical Italian style of the period, the makers have provided opening three-quarter light windows. The trouble is that the glued-on catches do not take long to become detached from the glass.

It seems particularly odd, in view of the emphasis placed on catering for the needs of the driver, that it is impossible for the man at the

wheel to get a clear view of the two most regularly used instruments. The speedometer and rev counter are hidden behind the rim of the wheel, which means the driver has to duck his head to look underneath.

Nevertheless, the driving position is first class, despite the lack of seat back adjustment, and a surprise in view of the normal Italian pre-

The Dino line up at an English meeting of various car clubs. This picture clearly shows the headlamp differences and the vulnerability of the bodywork

79

occupation with designing cars around models of people with (by British standards) abnormally short legs and long arms. Inside, everything is non-reflective matt, including the two windscreen wipers which operate towards the centreline in Tower Bridge fashion. At very high speed these windscreen wipers lift several inches from the screen when the car hits unevenness in the road or is struck by a gust of wind.

Vision to the front is perfect, as soon as the driver becomes accustomed to not being able to look out across a bonnet, but the view out of the slot of a rear screen is not so good. There are usually no exterior mirrors—how could there be on such a shape?—so the driver has to rely on the interior mirror, which gives a fine view of the bodywork hump that covers the air filter.

Access to that engine is poor, via a mere flap that allows the owner to check the oil level and three of the six spark plugs; the forward three have to be reached through a removable panel inside the car. The Dino is definitely not a car for the home mechanic, though service managers with all the right equipment (and know-how) say it is quite straightforward. For instance, to get at the ancillary drive belts requires removing a wheel and a panel and then tackling it from beneath. Once discovered, it is all quite easy, they say.

For a car that is alleged to have so much emphasis on driver comfort, the seat shaping is not so good. There is a hard ridge across the shoulders and no back adjustment. All the driver can easily do, without resorting to spanners, is to adjust the seat fore and aft. Otherwise, everything for the driver is fine—apart from being a shade too warm because of the lack of ventilation. Not that it is much good fiddling with the heating and ventilation controls. After a while they become frustratingly stiff to operate, and except in

By the time the radiator, spare wheel, brake servo and windscreen washer bottle are fitted there is no room left in the front of the Dino for anything other than a toothbrush.

deepest winter it is best to leave them on 'cool'.

All that metal thrashing about so close to the occupants' ears is bound to make the Dino noisy. However, to the true believer it is music.

The lights are rather ineffective, which can be alarming on a high-performance car, and while there is good space for two there is precious little room in the cockpit for anything else. Luggage space is reasonable, but its location to the rear of the engine means the owner's pyjamas and toothpaste are nicely warmed up on the journey! It is interesting to note that one of the Ferraris which came afterwards, the 308GT4, possessed a token rear seat like the model the 246 was designed to rival, the Porsche 911.

The ride is rather bobbly over secondary

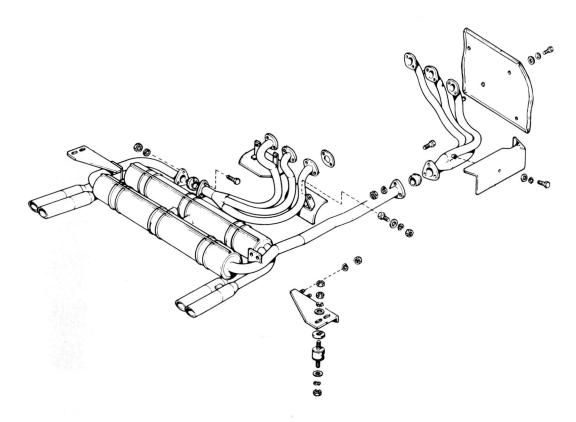

Two transverse silencers solved the problem of fitting an effective exhaust system to a mid-engined car

roads, but it flattens out as speed increases, and that, after all, is what the Dino is all about. Given its head, on a smooth, open road, the Dino is transformed. It seems content pottering about at low speeds in traffic, but it is not doing the engine any good—and besides, is that not sacrilege?

One other Italian characteristic which does manifest itself is the change into second gear when cold. In fact, a car left overnight, for instance, may simply refuse to engage second gear from first. It will oblige after a few miles, when the oil in the gearbox has warmed up sufficiently, but a good many Dino owners learn to live with the trait by doing a U-turn change from first to third gear.

This, then, was the Dino as seen by magazine readers. Road testers had been knocked in the aisles by the car's immaculate handling and sparkling performance. There were a few minor irritations, but nothing that could mar the joy to be derived from driving Enzo's baby.

Or were there? History and experience have revealed that owning a Dino Ferrari was not all hedonistic pleasure. They could be infuriatingly unreliable, and their lack of proper development soon became apparent in ownership.

'Anyone who buys a Dino for everday transport is in for a lot of expense,' says a specialist dealer. 'They make fantastic second cars— really great fun to drive despite all the speed

With such poor access to the engine, covers are essential to protect the bodywork during mechanical work on the Dino

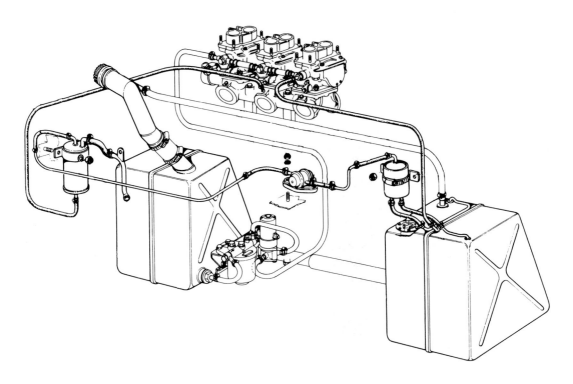

The Dino's fuel system was as complicated as the rest of the car. Two small tanks made economical use of the wing space. The recirculatory system ensured that there would be no vapour locks—a problem in some earlier Ferraris

restrictions. But it would be as well to have something a bit more reliable and economical in the garage. The Dino is terrific if properly maintained, it has a super gearbox and the handling is out of this world. It has extremely good brakes: driving it on the road, they will never fade, though they will if used on a circuit.'

For instance, it is part of motor industry folklore that Italian cars rust heavily and quickly, or at least they did until recently. The Ferrari Dino is no exception. The door sills and the wheel arches soon show the crust of brown ferrous oxide. There is a futher notable spot between the front wheel arches and the front of each door. It is double skinned, and once the water and salt and grit have got in, the only way out is *through* the metal. An experienced Ferrari technician like Jock Bruce, a director of Modena Engineering, can look at a Dino and tell from a distance whether there is a major rust problem simply by the way the front and rear bodywork hangs—or sags, to be more precise.

One owner, struggling to rebuild a cheap secondhand version, decided to have the bodywork cleaned up by abrasive blasting. The trouble was, it came back looking like lace, so little solid metal was left in it. None of this affects the structure of the car—it has a stout tubular chassis holding it together—and body panels are luckily still available. But it does underline the fact that renovating a cheap one is going to cost a lot of money.

Second gear on high mileage examples may become virtually unusable except by double declutching. It takes a tremendous loading, especially when cold, and the synchromesh has to work that bit harder. It often fails to work at all. One is left to wonder just how a company like Porsche would have tackled the problem, for it seems unlikely that many German motorists would be prepared to accept a defective piece of machinery in a car that costs so much.

The engine feels tremendously tractable, and content to potter around town at low engine speeds as well as flying on the ground. It will do so, but deep down it was not what it was designed for. Thus it will register its protest about such treatment by wearing down the high lift cam profiles—something that will cost in the region of £500 to replace. The alternative is to have the tappets adjusted over 6000 miles intervals, at a cost of something like £100.

It is vital that recommended maintenance is carried out at the proper intervals. And the labour content for each of these is a far cry from the plug-in check of modern-day production cars—six

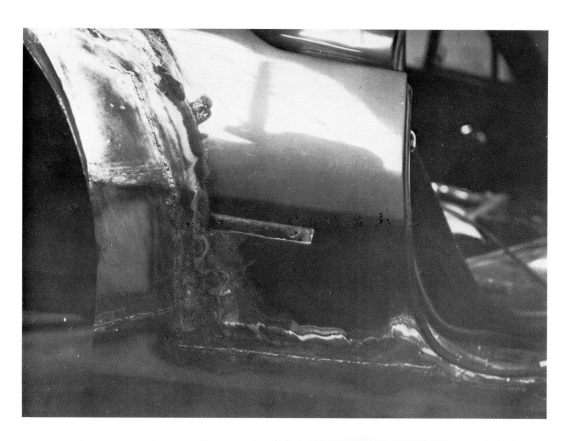

*When rust has taken hold of
the rear wheel arches the
only cure is to cut out and
weld in new metal. Here's
how*

*What shouldn't happen with
any car, let alone a Ferrari—
rust in the sills*

hours for the small (3000 miles) service, 15 hours for the medium (6000 miles) and 20 hours for the 12,000 miles major service.

Thus, in a year's motoring of around 12,000 miles, the owner will have to pay for 47 hours' worth of regular maintenance on a Dino. At a labour rate of (say) £9 an hour for a skilled mechanic, there amounts some £423. Then there is VAT and parts costs....

Electrics are another regular Dino problem. The twin coils of earlier models were replaced by a single dual purpose one after a short time. But running an engine at high speeds requires precise timing; any abnormal loading—a corroded ter-

Bodywork restoration must follow the methods used in original construction— welding and shaping

87

minal, for instance—can soon cause the system to fail. It is another example of the need for regular servicing.

A further oddity is that the Dino has two ignition systems. The Dinoplex electronic ignition made by Marelli is perfect for delivering the spark at the right time—while it works. The makers are clearly aware of the frailty of the unit, for they have thoughtfully provided a conventional system as well and a change-over switch to engage it.

All electrical gadgetry as far as the Dino was

concerned was further complicated when a fire at the factory held up supplies. Of course, this was nothing to do with the car itself, but the difficulty in obtaining subsequent spares shook an already doubtful reputation the car had for the reliability of its electrical components.

There is the leaking roof of the open GTS models. Driving along, there are numerous squeaks and groans from the Targa roof panel as its frame flexes around it. The windscreen surround, weakened by the deletion of the one-piece roof panel, moves about through a distance of some

This GTS bodyshell is well into restoration. Although an expensive operation, the 'perfect' car is well worth the effort. Many large motor manufacturers would consider Dino construction methods primitive

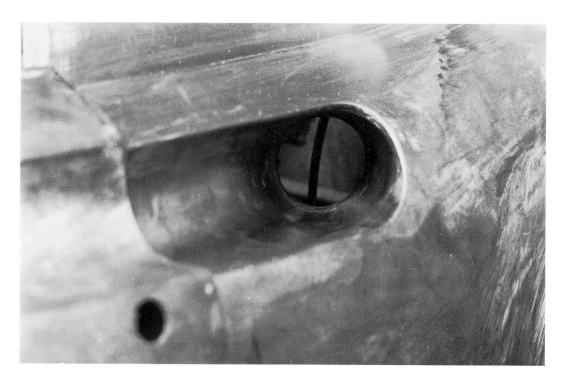

No mere styling gimmick; these enormous scoops ahead of the Dino's rear wings feed air to the engine compartment and with luck to the rear brakes. This car is undergoing restoration

eighth of an inch. This would be annoying enough on an inexpensive car, but when it manifests itself in the way it does, the owner of this costly car begins to wonder what he is paying for.

The interior is nicely trimmed in dark, non-reflective material, and very effective it looks too. The trouble is that the flexing roof panel allows rain water to drip through and onto the facia. It dries, leaving white stains that prove impossible to remove. Ferrari vendors have tried everything to remove or disguise them, including shoe polish, which precludes anyone actually touching the facia. The only cure, according to dealers, is to have the whole thing re-trimmed.

The Dino, then, may look a beauty from afar, but close companionship reveals plenty of warts. It is a throwback to the age when Ferraris were made for favoured customers. And that is despite the undoubted advances made following the arrival of Michael Parkes and the influence of Fiat.

In the old days, when road cars were simply adapted racing cars, the owner expected, or even wanted, compromise. But the Dino was not a racing model. It has no true track record of its own, and was created as a road car to fight for Porsche 911 sales. This was something new for Ferrari—a whole new dish of *gelato*.

The emphasis was still on engine and transmission, but the company had come a long way from this total preoccupation, and the remainder of the car was gradually rising to those standards. The Dino road cars thus represented a transition from the old craft methods to the early days of semi-industrialized production.

To that extent it can only be judged a qualified success. Those models which came afterwards were not as fickle as the early, curvy Dinos. They were still, to some extent, examples of Ferrari cashing in on its illustrious racing name—albeit the finest in the world—with a car that was not productionised. 'Oh, it went well and stopped well and it looked stupendous. But, and it is a major "but", the whole thing *was* rather underdeveloped.'

Who, for instance, but an Italian company could get away with manufacturing a low-production, supposedly sophisticated gearbox with a known weakness, and one that in one respect would not work at all under certain conditions? What other car maker, asking masses of money for the product, could get away with a car that leaked when it rained, and which had several well known water traps that could eventually lead to gaping rusty holes appearing in the sides?

Why build two ignition systems into the car, including a back-up one for a first set-up that was simply expected to fail? Would it not have been more logical in the long term to have developed a piece of equipment that would work without fuss the whole time?

The same with the camshaft wear problem. It takes a special kind of disregard, or arrogance, on

the part of any car maker to ignore weaknesses which are so well known. It may have been a standard that was acceptable a decade or more earlier, when all cars required servicing every 3000 miles or so, did need regular chassis lubrication, and did need the oil to be changed because it had been broken down by all that high-speed motoring. In this respect, the Dino was every bit an

Not Scaglietti's factory in Modena, Italy with a Dino under manufacture, but Graypaul Motors near Loughborough in England as yet another 246 undergoes ground-up restoration before it's even ten years old

echo of that earlier age, just as its body style would suggest.

Almost all other vehicle makers in the world, aided by advanced technology on the part of the component suppliers and the oil industry, were moving away from such frequent servicing intervals. It was not just for cheap economy cars either; Porsche were among the pioneers. The Stuttgart company's unitary steel construction model, older and more old-fashioned in mechanical layout, was moving towards annual services and a warranty on bodywork rust that lasted six years. Anything similar from the Italians would have spelled financial disaster for them.

That none of these faults was cured was in part due to the small volume—only just over 4000 altogether in the years they were offered for sale. Spreading the cost of any modifications over so few cars was prohibitively expensive. But for a small, flexible company it would surely not have been too much to ask, for instance, that the susceptible cam profiles were reworked, trading a longer life for a few horsepower. Then again, it did not take long for the flimsiness of the bodywork to become apparent after exposure to a couple of northern winters.

It was almost as if the capricious creator had his mind on other things. Yet the plans for the masterwork had been laid down, and all it needed was a little finishing development work of the type in which the German car makers excel. Instead, the raw creation was left—a reminder of the way in which the great Leonardo da Vinci would lay out a canvas, full of enthusiasm, only to become distracted by other projects. As a result, the world today has almost-completed Leonardos, just as the car world has plenty of almost-developed Ferrari road cars. It is just such a pity the job was not seen through to the end.

Chapter 7
What Was Achieved?

Did Ferrari learn from the Dino exercise? And, indeed, did it prove to be the right move for the company at the time? The answer can only be Yes, and there is little doubt a lot was learned in the process. Were a similar machine to be launched today—a less likely event in view of the world's preoccupation with energy awareness and the anti-social implications, however misguided, of two-seater sports cars capable of 150 mph—one with the flaws of the Dino would be hard-pressed to win sales, however beguiling the badge.

It is just that the very much higher levels of reliability and comfort and quality built into even mundane family cars these days have made the public more demanding. The foibles of luxury cars will be much harder to sell in a period of increasing consumer legislation such as that over product liability which has been simmering around EEC committees for several years now. If it ever reaches the statute book in some of its more demanding forms this will be a mighty tough law on many of the specialist car makers.

The Italians have an expression which could have been written with the Dino in mind, and with a longing eye on the day when cars will not cost so much to own: *Donne e motori—gioie e dolori*, or, women and cars give both pain and joy. (The Italian male, of course, still tends to hold male chauvinism in very high regard.)

But the Dino did lead the supercar makers into another field. It made a lot of sense to attract a fresh breed of customers—people with less money but ones who might eventually buy a true exotic at twice the price. Besides, there simply was not enough work to keep all those people employed turning out Daytonas or Boxers. So while they were waiting around to develop new cars of the type in which they excelled, and on which their reputation had been built, it made a

lot of sense for Ferrari to have the employees turning out little cars at half the price. It kept the lire—and the pounds and francs and dollars—coming in when times were a bit thin. For the UK importers, too, it was good business. Nearly 700 versions of the Dino were sold here, the most for any one model at that time.

Let's summarize the Dino as the first exploration of a new market—and one in which Ferrari thought aloud at the customer's expense.

The V6 Dino's true successor, Pininfarina's 308GTB of 1975 was labelled 'Ferrari' from the start. That superb beauty line lives on in this V8 engined car. Once again Ferrari pioneered—the first bodyshells were in glass fibre later returning to metal, and it's hard to tell which is which

The first Dino successor if not the 'true' one. Bertone's 308GT4 was a sophisticated machine showing more evidence of Fiat influence. The name Dino was dropped in 1976

The 308 which came after, although dismissed by many as not being a true Ferrari ('Good heavens, it even has toothed belt drive for its camshafts and everyone knows a Ferrari has gears and chain drive!'), was unquestionably more practical and reliable. Yet it was with considerable distaste that the early 308s were greeted. They had glass fibre bodies at first. Perhaps it was the company's answer to the rust problem experienced on the 246, though post-1973 308 models did return to use of steel.

Then again, the 308GT4 featured rear seats, however restricted they may have been. The

Porsche had always had them, and the Dino's two subsequent Italian rivals had them too. It was really more a question of Fiat—by then in production control—deciding that Ferrari should present some more sophisticated competition for the Porsche.

The Italian rivals emerged into the market place of 1972, just before the Dino 246 was replaced. They were the Lamborghini Urraco, a 220 bhp 2.5-litre V8, and the Maserati Merak, powered by the 3-litre 190 bhp V6 that the company had developed for use in the Citroën SM grand touring car. Interestingly, both of these

The Bertone-styled Fiat Dino coupé was praised for its clean and classic lines

99

140 mph cars offered (admittedly limited) space for small or occasional passengers, or for extra luggage. So, to this end, did the next Ferrari model out of the mould.

Pininfarina's Dino styling was another give-away to the limited career of the model. Bertone's Urraco and Giugiaro's Merak adopted the more formal straight lines and wedge shape that has proven so successful in motor racing. The Dino was a copy of a racing car that had been successful in the mid-1960s, and a great deal had

1969 saw this Fiat Dino cash in on Ferrari's reputation. In retrospect these Fiat Dinos are much better than they were first assessed

happened on the race tracks since then. It was no surprise, then, that when the Dino 308 by Bertone—his first for the company for many years—did appear, it should have the straighter lines that were becoming more commonplace. It featured a direct Urraco influence.

The Pininfarina Dino, on the other hand, could trace its links to the curves of cars like the Jaguar's racing D type or E type which were trend-setters of the time. Perhaps Pininfarina has never lost his love for such lines, for the recent

Pininfarina did something less than his best on the Fiat Dino spider. This 1968 version is a German Press demonstrator

styling exercise based on the Jaguar XJ-S, and seen at a number of motor shows, bears a strong resemblance to the balance and curves of earlier Jaguars.

Indeed, this harking back to the old styles may be one of the reasons for the Dino's high second-hand value at the time of writing. It may be a question of nostalgia. Anything—or at least so many things—from a by-gone age seems capable

of commanding such high prices in today's look-alike world of boring boxes and mass production. The same, of course, is true in other spheres, such as those of fashion and popular music.

For, make no mistake, the Dino is an appreciating asset. They cost just over £6200 when they were discontinued in the UK. Their poor reputation for reliability saw secondhand market values plummet, despite a well-earned reputation

This three-quarter rear view flatters the car's styling. The Fiat would provide Dino motoring for a reasonable price

for being something special in the way of styling and performance.

It was a bleak time economically too, but with the improvement in many peoples' personal wealth in the later 1970s, the value of the Dino staged a recovery. Today a mint example would realize nearly double its asking price when new, and there are not many vehicles as recent as the Dino of which this can be said.

There are enthusiasts scouring the land trying to find nice examples, but it is highly unlikely that they will strike gold. 'A bad Dino is worse than useless,' warns Jock Bruce succinctly. A Maranello Concessionaires' man says a potential buyer should be wary of anything costing under £6,000—and they should know as the official UK importers. A fully rebuilt body, for instance, would cost up to £5,000. A new engine would cost a similar amount. Clearly there are few bargains— and plenty of potential headaches—in the field of used Dinos.

It is difficult to know where to place the Dino in importance in the overall historical perspective. Will historians in fifty years' time look back on the Dino and declare that it was the ultimate statement of the age, as many people now believe? Or will it be forgotten? It certainly will not be by enthusiasts, even if the 1960s and 1970s must surely go down as the age of the mass-produced car, when more and more people in the western world aspired to car ownership. For them, the need was cheap, reliable motoring from A to B, a need fulfilled, and fuelled, at ever-increasing fever pitch by a dwindling group of vehicle makers whose influence and tentacles began to embrace the world.

In such context the Dino was an irrelevance, an anachronism. It was a leftover from an age that was, for so many people, a better one. It was like a

naughty deed in a good, sanitized world. It did not represent the end of the line for cars like this, but it appeared in an era when there was an increasing revulsion for cars that were flagrant transgressors of speed limits. Indeed, there were many people, in America in particular, who regarded personal transport for just two people in a world where natural resources are finite, as being downright antisocial.

Very definitely a Fiat with little Ferrari influence— conservative thinking

The heart of the matter; Ferrari's race-bred Dino engine, seen here in the Fiat-produced iron block version mated to the Fiat Dino transmission

But it will have a small place in motoring history, perhaps even in the history of art if the Futurists are correct. Perhaps Ferrari will be celebrated with an exhibition of his work, as was the Bugatti family in London in the autumn of 1979. They were fascinating shapes, reflections on a small section of a wealthy world that witnessed the spread of mass production and a slump of unprecedented proportions.

What the Dino did for Ferrari was to establish the pattern for today. The ostensible reason for its creation, though, to go racing in Formula 2, was an unmitigated failure.

Ferrari no longer relies on the sales of ultra-fast twelve-cylinder models as it once did to support its motor racing. Today, the pocket money is handed out by the accountants in Turin.

When it was decided to go ahead with production in the middle and late 1960s, the company was, like all the world's car makers, unaware of the chaos that would reign in the energy field, the vehicle safety requirements and the exhaust emission regulations. Had those decisions not been taken then—even though they were for different reasons—Ferrari could have found itself in an exceedingly embarrassing position. As it is, by the time the crunch came they were already within the Fiat fold, which to a great extent was to cushion the men of Maranello.

It is unlikely the Dino ever made much in the way of profits. After all, as every manufacturer knows, just because a car is half the price of another and contains six cylinders instead of twelve, the costs of producing it are not halved. In some areas its cost are virtually the same, and the only real savings are often in the amount of materials used or when producing engine components in multiples of six rather than twelve.

Just how much the Dino did earn for the company will probably never be known. But there seems little doubt that in its role of bringing together Fiat and Ferrari, the Dino enabled Ferrari to go on making road cars, and making them better than they ever had in the past. To that extent, the Dino was the model that ensured Enzo Ferrari's future as a manufacturer.

Appendix
A New Star Joins the Studio

The Dino 246 may have gone, but at least one part of it lived on. There has been a good deal of cross-fertilization between the previously independent members of the giant Fiat group, but as yet there has been only one example of a major Ferrari product being used elsewhere in the group under a different marque name. That example is the Lancia Stratos, the striking mid-engined two-seater which dominated world rallying in the mid-1970s. At its heart was that Dino V6 engine and transmission.

It was a unique marriage of Lancia and Ferrari, and an incredibly successful one, devised by Fiat to help rejuvenate the Lancia company whose first Fiat-based models were going on sale in Europe. The Stratos—a wedge-shaped supercar in every way—was largely responsible for creating the present Lancia public image of performance, sophistication and quality.

The Stratos story deserves telling separately at greater length, but an outline of its career is especially relevant to the Ferrari Dino since the V6 saw some of its most exciting developments when installed in the works Stratos rally cars. By their very nature, rally cars are ones that can be used on the road, so the Lancia occupies an unequal position in the sport by being a car that was designed from the very start as a competition vehicle with use on the public roads only of

*1970 Turin Show—Bertone
showed this 'pre'-Stratos*

1971 Turin Show—the Stratos proper must be the ultimate expression of the wedge-shaped car

incidental importance. How very different to the car from which it borrowed the engine!

Those who have driven the Stratos confirm that its lack of any compromises in favour of everyday use makes it temperamental even by supercar standards.

In fact, the Stratos began life as a styling exercise by that man Bertone again. It was first

When first used by Bertone as a styling exercise the engine was Lancia's own fine Fulvia V4

shown at the Turin Motor Show of 1970; rarely can one of these extravagant styling fantasies seen so often at Turin have been developed so far and so fast. At that time the car used a V4 Lancia Fulvia engine and running gear, fitted like the Dino in the mid-engine position. It was noticed by the then team manager for Lancia, Cesare Fiorio, whose imagination was captured by its striking

Right *Taken from the
production Stratos driver's
handbook this picture shows
the cockpit. 1 Water
temperature, 2 Ammeter,
3 Oil pressure, 4 Oil
temperature, 5 Brake fluid
indicator, 6 Tachometer,
7 Speedometer, 8 Hand
throttle, 9 Choke,
10 Handbrake, 11 Fuel,
12 Throttle pedal, 13 Brake
pedal, 14 Clutch pedal,
15 Direction indicator,
16 Light switch, 17 Dip
switch*

Far right *Perhaps the car
which persuaded Lancia into
productionizing the
Stratos—both on the race
track and in rallies the
Alpine A110 was pretty
successful. This is a rare shot
of one on the Targa Florio in
1973*

looks and by its potential as a competition vehicle
for Lancia, at that time a dominant force in
rallying. But the Fulvia was becoming quickly
out-paced by more specialist cars from other
companies.

The Stratos was not such an unlikely prospect,
for sports cars like the Porsche 911 and Alpine-
Renault were coming to the fore, and other
companies were experimenting with two-seaters,
most notably Ford with their ill-fated GT70. But
one thing was clear—that the 1600 cc V4 engine of
the Fulvia HF would not be powerful enough to
make the Stratos a winner. And by then Lancia had
no other engines themselves. But, being part of the
Fiat group, there were other possibilities. One was
the 2-litres Abarth-developed Fiat twin-cam. The
other was the Fiat-made Dino V6.

Clearly, the choice was subject to intense
political machinations within the group, and

some clever lobbying by Fiorio. However, the involvement of Fiat in their own rally programme with the 124 Spider and the sheer suitability of the Dino unit—already mid-mounted in the Ferrari—made the final choice inevitable.

The Stratos appeared in road-going form with the Dino V6 at the 1971 Turin Motor Show. Italy's very handy lack of legislation governing the construction of new cars gave Lancia an enviable

The skeletal nature of the Stratos is emphasized in this rear end view—a 'conventional' 12-valve rally car. Its noise never goes unnoticed

freedom in designing the car. Its basis was a very strong central structure with outriggers to the front, holding the wishbone front suspension and the engine/gearbox unit slung behind, between the rear suspension struts. Everything was designed for easy adjustment and repair in the field—quite unlike the Ferrari. The Stratos was a racing car going rallying, and could be set up with racing precision to suit the prevailing conditions.

Although obviously a rally car this Stratos is 'plain Jane' without spoilers, lamp mouldings and other paraphernalia

Development problems being discussed at the Casale race track in September 1974— Claudio Maglioli in the helmet, Mike Parkes to his left

During 1972—when the Dino 246 was being wound down and the 308 was on its way—development and testing continued before the car made its first competition appearance near the end of the year in the Tour de Corse where it was handled by Sandro Munari, one of the world's leading drivers and a person who, in the coming years, was to become synonymous with the Stratos. The car did not last long—it was still very much under development—but in 1973 Munari used the Stratos along with a Fulvia to win the European Rally Championship, scoring two wins with the Ferrari-powered car.

At the end of 1973 Mike Parkes—a person who has cropped up before in this story—joined the Lancia competitions department as a development engineer. It was largely thanks to him that the Stratos leaped to prominence in the next two years, and developed so quickly into a reliable, rapid competition car.

Initial development work on the Dino engine in its competition Lancia form soon saw power approaching 250 bhp, an increase of nearly thirty per cent on the Dino road car. It involved modifications to the camshafts, compression ratio and carburation. But even this was not considered enough for some competition use, so radical developments were planned to improve output still more.

Parkes masterminded two major projects—the development of a four valves-per-cylinder engine, and turbocharging. When he joined the team the four-valve motor was already under development but was proving unreliable. In less than a year it was to become the mainstay of the works effort.

The potential of turbocharging was never fully explored. A Stratos Turbo appeared on a Tour de France and, intermittently, in Group 5 sports car racing, but without success. Lancia's whole effort was going into rallying, and, besides, Group 5 circuit racing was proving an expensive failure as a major spectator draw. Turbocharging, then, had to go into the pending file.

It was not until October 1974 that the Stratos was officially homologated into Group 4 and allowed into international competition. It had previously run as a prototype at the discretion of the organizers. By the end of the following month it had, incredibly, made Lancia World Rally Champions. The season had had a late start because of the fuel crisis, and in October and November five rounds were packed in.

Lancia entered the first, the San Remo, with a plan to do more if they were successful. When Munari gave the car a win the first time out the team set off for the two North American rounds; Munari won again in a four valve car in Canada, but the Stratos broke down in the United States. He came to the RAC Rally of Great Britain needing points to consolidate the championship position and, after leading in the four-valve car, finished a careful third. Final round was the Tour de Corse and, though Munari's car dropped a valve, Jean-Claude Andruet's Stratos won to clinch the championship.

The following year (1975) was all-Stratos. It opened with the Monte Carlo where Munari scored the first of what was to become a straight hat-trick of wins. But in a year when the Stratos dominated rallying, it was two failures which earned it its greatest glory. The first was on the East African Safari, a long, dusty marathon that seemed quite absurd for the tiny little Stratos to tackle. But Lancia were determined, Parkes and Munari spent an enormous amount of time testing before the rally, strengthening the car and developing Safari suspension. A massive 'roo bar dominated the wedge nose, and spares were

Cesare Fiorio masterminded Lancia's 'Dino' attack with the Stratos making it perhaps Lancia's most successful competition car ever

Better engine access than a Dino—a conventional 12-valve Stratos engine

carried on a rack above the engine hatch. It was all to no avail. Both team cars were bedevilled by problems, ranging from punctures to an incident with a local car. They could only manage second and third places.

In the RAC Rally that November, Bjorn Waldegard showed just how shatteringly quickly a Stratos could be driven on un-practised loose surfaces, always thought its weakest element. He

The Stratos turbocharged engine as used by Sandro Munari on the 1974 Tour de France

set forty best times on the seventy-two stages, but again to no avail. A broken driveshaft put the car out of time early in the event and disqualification was inevitable.

The world championship was Lancia's for a third time in 1976, when four-valve cars finished first, second and third in Monte Carlo, though the Safari effort once more ended in failure. But even at the height of its power, the writing was on the

Above *24-valves and carbon fibre bodywork for this Giro d'Italia car, but still the Dino 246 script on the cambox covers*

Right *Sadly no more! Stratos leads Fulvia on the Targa Florio, 1973*

wall for the Stratos. Rule changes were set to ban its four-valve heads from 1978—items that had been homologated as 'extras' to the original car and no longer to be permitted.

The four valve version of the Dino engine had given the Stratos its tremendous advantage over the opposition. Lancia claimed as much as 320 bhp, though slightly less than 300 bhp might be a more widely accepted figure. None the less, it was nearly sixty-five per cent more than when installed in the Dino, and between ten and fifteen

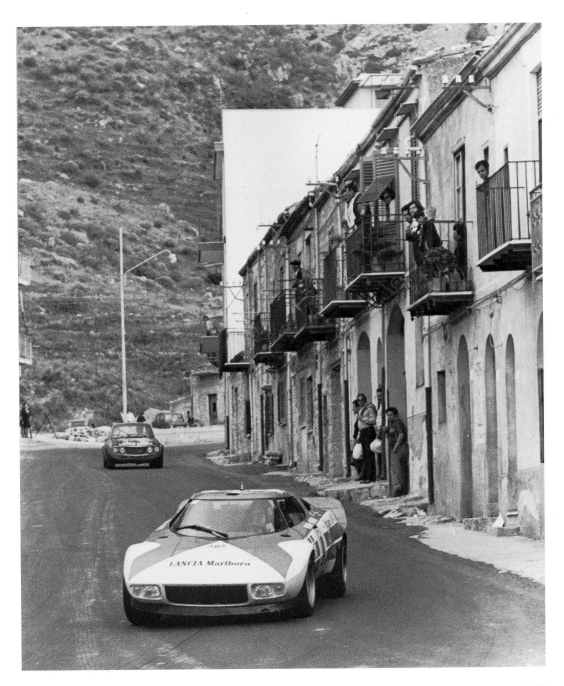

One of a number of very
specially equipped Stratos
used to tackle the Safari
Rally. Lancia proved that
they could tie the car together
sufficiently well to enable it
to last the distance. In truth
the chassis was so over
engineered in the beginning
that they needed to do little
but glue the bodywork
together. Although they
never won this African event
they were often front runners.
Here's Munari during the
1976 event—on this occasion
his engine failed

per cent more than any of the rally opposition. It also had a more usable torque curve than that of the two-valve engine. Only the works teams used the four-valve motors, incidentally. The many semi-works and private teams, including the London-based Chequered Flag, were restricted to two valve engines.

In 1976 the Fiat management decided that their exotic car domination of rallying should come to an end, and a so-called production car

should take over the quest for the World Championship. So the Fiat Abarth 131 became the contender in 1977 (and won) and the Stratos was restricted to a few prestige outings.

Development work on the two-valve engine continued so that it would be able to power the works cars from 1978, but there was less sense of urgency. Stratos production has stopped—with a few hundred cars built in all—so homologation would soon run out. Tragically, Mike Parkes was

This time the Stratos shows considerable development with extended wheel arches, roof 'wing' and headlamp pod. On this 1979 event, the Giro d'Italia, Tony Carello won group 4. Is that a rear wheel off the road?

127

then killed in a car crash, and with his death development faltered still more.

The two-valve engine in the Lancia was no slouch in its final guise, producing some 270 bhp at 7600 rpm and 199 lb ft of torque at 600 rpm. It ran on an 11:1 compression ratio and usually retained Weber carburation, though petrol injection was tried on occasion.

The works two-valve car won just a single World Championship rally in 1978, the San Remo. Its works career came to an end at the finish of that season, though a single car was allowed out of

The ultimate Stratos? Probably not for there is still competition life left—24-valve engine and carbon fibre bodywork. Lancia made much more of the Dino engine in this car than Ferrari did in their roadsters

retirement for the 1979 RAC Rally.

It was a short but meteoric career in world rallying, yet one that will not be quickly forgotten by enthusiasts. The magical sing-song warble above the roar of the exhausts—apparently caused by harmonics of the camshafts inside the cam boxes—will remain a memory to anyone who witnessed a works four-valve car in full flight and the images of the tiny wedge sliding through the sunlit snowbanks of Monte Carlo or struggling overburdened through the *murram* of Africa have become part of motor sport's history.

Perhaps some of the most exciting graphics have appeared on both Ferraris and Lancias, now both under the Fiat wing

Specifications

	206GT	246GT (GTS)
Years of production	1967–69	1969–74 (1972–74)
Number built	150	2732 (1180)

Engine

No of cylinders	6 in 65° vee	6 in 65° vee
Bore × stroke	85 × 57 mm	92.5 × 60 mm
Capacity	1987 cc	2418 cc
Cylinder heads	light alloy	light alloy
Cylinder block	light alloy	cast iron
Compression ration	9.0:1	9.0:1
Valve gear	2 ohc per bank	2 ohc per bank
No of main bearings	4	4
Carburettor	3 × Weber 40DCF	3 × Weber 40DCF
Ignition	Dinoplex	Dinoplex
Sump capacity	12 pints	14 pints
Power/engine speed	180 bhp/8000 rpm	195 bhp/7600 rpm
Torque/engine speed		165.5 lb ft/5500 rpm

Transmission

Clutch	single dry plate	single dry plate
Gearbox	5-speed, reverse	5-speed, reverse
Differential	limited slip	limited slip

Specifications

Chassis	tubular steel frame	tubular steel frame
Body	light alloy	steel
Suspension front	unequal length wishbones, coil springs, anti-roll bar	unequal length wishbones, coil springs, anti-roll bar
rear	unequal length wishbones, coil springs, anti-roll bar	unequal length wishbones, coil springs, anti-roll bar

Brakes	servo-assisted dual circuit	servo-assisted dual circuit
front	11 in vent. disc	11 in vent. disc
rear	10.5 in vent. disc	10.5 in vent. disc
Steering	rack and pinion	rack and pinion
Wheels	$14 \times 6\frac{1}{2}$J alloy	$14 \times 6\frac{1}{2}$J alloy
Tyres	185×14	205×14
Fuel tank capacity	13.5 Imp. gall	14.5 Imp. gall

Dimensions

Wheelbase	90 in	92.3 in
Length	163 in	166.7 in
Width	67 in	67.2 in
Height	42 in	45 in
Weight	1984 lb	2380 lb

Performance

Speed in 1st	N/A	40 mph
Speed in 2nd	N/A	60 mph
Speed in 3rd	N/A	85 mph
Speed in 4th	N/A	112 mph
Maximum speed	140 mph	150 mph
0–50 mph	5.6 sec	5.7 sec
0–60 mph	7.5 sec	6.8 sec
0–70 mph	9.8 sec	9.5 sec
0–80 mph	12.2 sec	12.2 sec
0–90 mph	15.3 sec	14.8 sec
0–100 mph	19.0 sec	18.0 sec
0–110 mph	24.0 sec	23.3 sec
0–120 mph	30.6 sec	29.5 sec

Acknowledgements

Generous co-operation came from many sources for the compilation of this book—both author and publishers extend their grateful thanks.

Firstly we would like to thank the factory (Ferrari Automobili SpA) at Modena and their British importers Maranello Concessionaires Limited through Mark Konig. Ferrari Owners Club 'jack of all trades' Godfrey Eaton lent a hand and David Clarke of Graypaul Motors and Jock Bruce at Modena Engineering did some hard talking. Then there was Jerrold Sloniger, Andrew Bell, Dudley Mason-Styrron, Geoffrey Goddard, Michael Frostick, Andrew Andersz of Lancia (England) Limited, Martin Holmes, Peter Roberts, Nigel Snowdon and Diana Burnett, *Autosport*, Tim Parker Collection, Gerry Stream, Carrozzeria Pininfarina, Carrozzeria Bertone, Franco Zagari, London Art Technical, Charles Pocklington, Neill Bruce, Andrew Morland, Paul Kunkel and Nicky Wright—and in no particular order. Thank you all.

Index